The History of Conservation
Preserving Our Planet

A Global Threat
The Emergence of
Climate Change Science

Avery Elizabeth Hurt

Cavendish
Square

New York

Published in 2018 by Cavendish Square Publishing, LLC
243 5th Avenue, Suite 136, New York, NY 10016

Copyright © 2018 by Cavendish Square Publishing, LLC

First Edition

Website: cavendishsq.com

This publication represents the opinions and views of the author based on
his or her personal experience, knowledge, and research. The information
in this book serves as a general guide only. The author and publisher have
used their best efforts in preparing this book and disclaim liability rising
directly or indirectly from the use and application of this book.

All websites were available and accurate when this book was sent to press.

Library of Congress Cataloging-in-Publication Data

Names: Hurt, Avery Elizabeth, author.
Title: A global threat: the emergence of climate change science / Avery Elizabeth Hurt.
Description: New York : Cavendish Square Publishing, 2018 |

Series: The history of conservation: preserving our planet |
Includes bibliographical references and index. | Audience: Grades 9-12.
Identifiers: ISBN 9781502631220 (library bound) | ISBN 9781502631237 (ebook)
Subjects: LCSH: Climatic changes--Juvenile literature. |
Global warming--Juvenile literature.
Classification: LCC QC903.15 H87 2018 | DDC 363.738'74--dc23

Editorial Director: David McNamara
Editor: Kristen Susienka
Copy Editor: Rebecca Rohan
Associate Art Director: Amy Greenan
Designer: Lindsey Auten
Production Coordinator: Karol Szymczuk
Photo Research: J8 Media

Printed in the United States of America

TABLE OF CONTENTS

Introduction 5

Chapter 1 11
Studying the Climate: From the Ice Age to the Greenhouse

Chapter 2 29
The Twenty-First Century:
From Measurements to Predictions

Chapter 3 51
The World Reacts

Chapter 4 71
Problems Facing Climate Change Action Today

Chapter 5 87
It's Late, but Not Too Late

Glossary 98

Further Information 100

Bibliography... 103

Index.. 108

About the Author... 112

Introduction

Everyone is talking about climate change these days—either to warn us that we're running out of time to address the problem and stave off its dreadful consequences or to assure us that all such warnings are silly at best and at worst a cruel hoax designed to cripple Western economies. Sometimes it can seem like global warming is just the latest "thing," as if someone noticed a few years ago that Earth's climate is warming up, and everyone suddenly started running around like Chicken Little saying, "The sky is falling!" However, climate science is anything but new. It is older than the computer, the atomic bomb, and antibiotics. In fact, people have been studying Earth's climate since before we had transatlantic flight or knew what DNA was. Far from being Chicken Little, the scientists who are warning us about it are some of the most cautious, level-headed people on this planet.

Checking and Double-Checking

The story of the science of climate change begins in the first half of the nineteenth century, with men (in those days scientists were almost all men) trying to understand the natural temperature swings of the planet. They hiked in the Swiss Alps, paying close attention to the patterns left in rocks as glaciers retreated. As

Opposite: This satellite image of the northeastern United States and southeastern Canada at night gives a brilliant demonstration of how much energy we use today.

more and more scientists began to study Earth's climate, they took to the sea to check the temperatures of the world's oceans. They invented machines that could detect small amounts of gases in the atmosphere. They drilled into the ice sheets of Greenland and the Antarctic to take samples of the air pockets trapped there. They developed computer programs that could predict with remarkable accuracy the effects on the climate of things such as volcanic eruptions and deforestation.

In the manner of all good science, they looked carefully at the evidence they found, gathered reams of data, then went back to the lab to evaluate that evidence, test that data, and apply rigorous scientific method and logic to their research. They discussed their findings with colleagues, who tested the results themselves. They published papers, which were also discussed and analyzed by other scientists. Then they went back and gathered more evidence and collected more data. They were surprised at what they found—that the planet was warming much more quickly than could be accounted for by the factors that had influenced the planet's temperature cycles for millennia. They were even more surprised when the evidence strongly suggested that the reason for this warming was that, since the Industrial Revolution, humans had been putting an unprecedented amount f carbon dioxide and other gases into the air by burning fossil els, such as coal and petroleum. Because they were scientists, y checked and rechecked their findings. Human-caused global ming was an important discovery, and they took plenty of to be absolutely sure they were right before they were willing it their scientific reputations behind it. In the end, there o denying it: global warming was happening—virtually entists agreed—and the primary cause of it was human behavior. If nothing was done to reverse this trend, the results could be catastrophic.

Bringing the Bad News

Like all good tales, the story of climate science has its share of conflict. When scientists began to warn the world of the problem, they discovered that some very powerful and very rich people were not happy to get the news (though it turned out that some of them were doing research on their own and already had the news!). Addressing the problem of human-caused global warming meant cutting back on the use of fossil fuels and replacing them with sources of energy that did not add to the increasing temperatures. Companies that made their money by selling fossil fuels would either have to sell less of their product and therefore make less money or figure out ways to make money selling energy sources that would be less harmful to the climate. Instead, they began a deliberate and detailed program of denying the science behind climate change, confusing the public, and convincing politicians and policymakers that it would be in their best interest to do nothing about what scientists were increasingly demonstrating was a crisis.

This was unfortunate, not only because it dangerously narrowed the window of time humans have to address the problem, but also because it prevented people from having real and honest debates. Though it is absolutely clear that Earth is warming dangerously fast and that human actions are the cause, many questions remain about the best way to address the problem without harming individuals, businesses, or the world's economies, and there is a great need for fresh ideas.

The good news—and there really is a lot of good news on this issue—is that while some people were working very hard to

Ordinary people are doing a lot to help slow down global warming. Things like riding bikes instead of driving or taking cabs can make a big difference.

keep the public from knowing and understanding the seriousness of the problem, others were trying just as hard to let the public know the truth, to put the evidence before them, and share with them the science so that they could see for themselves and make the decisions they felt were best based on the facts.

These days, most people are aware of how serious the problem is and how urgent it is that we act. Many people are working in ways large and small to try to help, from using less energy in their homes to marching in the streets to letting their leaders know how much this matters. But it all started more than 150 years ago, when a few underfunded scientists began wondering why Earth's temperature stayed—most of the time—not too hot and not too cold, but just right. Here is the exciting story of how scientists discovered the facts of climate change, struggled to get that information to the public, and how ordinary people are now working together to stop global warming before it really is too late.

1

Studying the Climate: From the Ice Age to the Greenhouse

L ouis Agassiz spent most of his days looking at fish fossils. In 1836, he was a professor of natural history at the University of Neuchâtel in Switzerland, where he specialized in classifying fishes. One summer, while vacationing in the Jura Mountains near his home, he took a close look at the glaciers there, and it changed his life—and the history of science.

Footprints of Glaciers

The observations Agassiz made that summer in the mountains weren't exactly new. Johann von Charpentier, a German-Swiss geologist, had already noticed **moraines**, the shapes of rocks, and scratches in the rocks that suggested glaciers had once come much farther south and then retreated (actually, this evidence was pointed out to him by a mountaineer named Jean-Pierre Perraudin), and hypothesized that all of Switzerland had been at

Opposite: Tropical forests help keep Earth's climate within a range that can support life as we know it.

The marks left by retreating glaciers were the first clues that Earth's climate had not always been as warm as it is now.

one time covered in ice. Like most scientists at the time, Agassiz didn't take this idea too seriously. In those days, it was generally accepted that this geological pattern was evidence of the great flood mentioned in Genesis, the first book of the Bible.

However, that summer Agassiz examined the evidence for himself and was utterly convinced that ice had once come much farther down. He continued to make observations and collect data. In the coming summers, he carefully measured the flow of melting glaciers and how glaciers moved; he traveled to other European countries and eventually to North America to study the evidence of past glaciation. Eventually, he argued that at one time Earth had been covered with glaciers from the North Pole to the Mediterranean. He called this the Eiszeit (German for "ice time"), and we now call it the Ice Age. Though it took him many years to convince the rest of the scientific community of this idea, and many of his details were wrong and had to be sorted out later through further research by Agassiz and other scientists, this was the first time that people realized that Earth's climate was not static, but had changed—dramatically—over time. Scientists eventually discovered that Earth had cycled in and out of ice ages for more than two million years. A long period when much of Earth was covered in ice would be followed by a much shorter period of warmer temperatures, then return to another ice age.

What Caused the Change?

Once people understood that Earth's climate was not stable over time, they began to try to work out what caused these changes.

fact!

Scientists have been taking detailed measurements of carbon dioxide in the atmosphere continuously for more than fifty years.

Perhaps it was variations in the heat of the sun? Volcanic eruptions could blanket the atmosphere in clouds of smoke, blocking the sun and cooling Earth. As mountain ranges rise and erode, wind patterns and ocean currents are altered. These were all pieces of the puzzle, but they did not explain enough. Meanwhile, other scientists in many different countries were also working on questions about Earth's climate.

Some were trying to figure out not so much why the climate changed, but why it did not change even more radically than it did. In the 1820s, a French scientist named Joseph Fourier began to ponder what could make a planet like Earth maintain a more or less constant average temperature. Fourier knew that heated surfaces emit heat energy. If Earth didn't emit the heat from the sun back into the atmosphere, the planet would soon be too hot to sustain life. On the other hand, he realized, there had to be something keeping some of the warmth in; otherwise Earth would freeze. Some kind of system must be keeping Earth in the Goldilocks zone—not too hot and not too cold, but just right—to support the kinds of life we know and depend on. Fourier reasoned that if Earth did not have an atmosphere, all the heat from the sun would escape, leaving Earth much colder. Earth's atmosphere, he explained, acts like a blanket trapping heat. Fourier used the analogy of a box with a glass lid on the top to describe this effect, something we now call the "greenhouse effect."

Scientists continued to work on the problem, and in 1862, John Tyndall, an English physicist, came up with a technique for measuring the effects that Fourier had surmised. He developed an apparatus that could accurately measure the heat-trapping abilities of various gases. Using this instrument, he discovered that water and carbon dioxide (CO_2) were two of the main gases that trap heat in Earth's atmosphere (what we now call greenhouse gases). Without water vapor, said Tyndall, Earth's surface would be "held fast in the iron grip of frost." CO_2 (or carbonic acid, as Tyndall called it), was second only to water vapor in its ability to trap heat. This was a key step in figuring out how the greenhouse effect worked.

In 1895, Swedish scientist Svante Arrhenius worked out that by adding carbon dioxide to the atmosphere by burning fossil fuels, such as coal, humans were raising Earth's average temperature. According to his calculations, if the amount of carbon dioxide in the atmosphere was doubled, it would lead to an average global temperature increase of 3 to 4 degrees Celsius (5 to 7 degrees Fahrenheit)—not too far off current estimates.

fact!

Every year for the past forty years has been warmer than the twentieth-century average.

Most people had trouble imagining humans were capable of having a significant effect on the climate of the planet. Sure, they understood that human activities might have some *local* effect on the weather. People had long suspected that cutting down lots of trees could influence rainfall amounts, but changes on a global scale seemed far too great to be a result of human activity. One man, however, noticed something else that supported Arrhenius's idea.

Guy Stewart Callendar was a steam engineer and a talented amateur climatologist who had been born in Canada but at the time was working in England. Callendar gathered temperature readings for most of the previous century from over one hundred weather stations scattered around the planet. He combined these readings to get an average global temperature for each year, doing all the calculations with pencil and paper. He published his findings in 1938. This data showed that the planet's average temperature had increased during that period, and he calculated that about half of that increase was due to increased carbon dioxide in the atmosphere. At the time, Callendar actually thought this was a good thing. It would delay the next ice age, said Callendar, perhaps indefinitely. He was right about that, but unfortunately, he did not know how much humanity's use of fossil fuels would increase in the coming years. The increase in greenhouse gases that had prevented the next ice age would soon go far beyond that to create an entirely new climatological age. They would push the climate from heading back toward being dangerously cold toward being dangerously warm.

Better Instruments, Better Data

Even if most scientists weren't yet convinced that the climate was rapidly warming and at least some of that was due to human activity, Callendar's data got their attention. More people began to work on the issue, and they were using increasingly better techniques and instruments. Governments began providing funding for climate science, in part because militaries needed information about weather, but also because climate change is likely to have a very big effect on international relations. Wars are often fought over limited resources, and the effects of climate change include droughts and famines, as well as other natural disasters.

By the 1950s, however, few scientists were concerned about the amount of CO_2 being added to the atmosphere by humans burning fossil fuels. Most people thought that the oceans would absorb any excess. In 1957, Roger Revelle, who was director of the Scripps Institute of Oceanography in La Jolla, California,

Roger Revelle (pictured here) demonstrated that the oceans did not absorb greenhouse gases quickly enough to prevent global warming.

and an expert on the interactions of the molecules in seawater, and Hans Suess, an Austrian-born American geochemist and nuclear physicist, discovered that the oceans absorbed CO_2 at a much slower rate than was previously thought. Human-generated emissions were indeed building up in the atmosphere and creating a greenhouse effect. Their findings were alarming. In a paper they published explaining their research, Revelle wrote, "human beings are now carrying out a large scale geophysical experiment of a kind that could not have happened in the past nor be reproduced in the future. Within a few centuries we are returning to the atmosphere and oceans the concentrated organic carbon stored in sedimentary rocks over hundreds of millions of years." He also wrote that the amount of gas in the atmosphere "may become significant during future decades if industrial fuel combustion continues to rise **exponentially**." Of course, industrial fuel combustion did indeed rise exponentially in the following decades—and it is rising still.

To get hard data and exact measurements of the carbon dioxide concentrations in the atmosphere, Revelle hired Charles David Keeling, a young geochemist who had recently developed a device that could detect carbon dioxide in very small quantities. Keeling, who was also known for his exactness and attention to detail, set up monitoring stations in La Jolla; Antarctica; and Mauna Loa, Hawaii—places where there were fewer factories and other sources of carbon dioxide to affect the measurements.

In 1960, Keeling made his first report. As expected, random local variations in concentrations of gases made the measurements from La Jolla unreliable. However, the data from Mauna Loa and Antarctica were impressive. In Antarctica, rising levels of carbon dioxide supported Revelle's hypothesis that fossil carbon was accumulating in the atmosphere. The data from Mauna Loa was even more interesting. There, the levels of carbon dioxide in the atmosphere showed a regular and distinct seasonal rise and

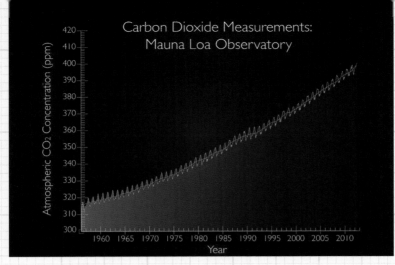

The dramatic message of the Keeling Curve motivated many scientists to further study the problem of Earth's changing atmosphere.

The Keeling Curve

The Keeling Curve (pictured above) is one of the most famous images in climate science. It shows the increase of carbon dioxide in Earth's atmosphere continually since the 1950s. The jagged part of the line represents the seasonal ups and downs—with more CO_2 in the atmosphere during the cooler winter months when plants are less active, and less atmospheric CO_2 in the warm summer months when there are more plants to take carbon dioxide out of the air. The overall trend of the pattern, however, is up—and not in a straight diagonal line from left to right. Notice how the line is not straight but curved. This is because not only is the amount of CO_2 in the atmosphere increasing over time, but the *rate* of increase of CO_2 is becoming greater as well. This is the image that alarmed Keeling and so many other climate scientists.

fall—Keeling had measured the fluctuations of carbon dioxide as it was taken out of the air by plants, which were more active in the warm seasons and more quiet in the cool ones. It was as if the planet itself were breathing in and out, just like an individual organism. Exciting as that was, the overall pattern was disturbing. While the seasonal changes reflect the natural cycles as plants flourish in warm weather and become dormant in cold weather, the data clearly showed that the *total* amount of carbon dioxide in the air was increasing. This was obvious from just three years of taking measurements. These results were enough to warrant longer-term monitoring.

For a brief period in 1964, Keeling lost his funding and was unable to take measurements, but excepting those few months, the measurement has been taken without interruption ever since 1958. Over all the years since, the seasonal variations and the trend toward increasingly higher concentrations of greenhouse gases have continued. The most alarming thing about Keeling's curve is that not only is carbon dioxide increasing, but the *rate of increase* is growing as well, as is shown by the sharp upward bend to the curve on the graph. With each passing year, the amount of carbon in the air increases by more than it did the year before. Scientists now have other ways of measuring the amount of carbon released into the atmosphere (including taking samples from air pockets in polar ice, which can show what carbon dioxide levels were in the distant past), but Keeling's readings of CO_2 levels are still a primary source of information about climate change. When you add Keeling's data to the now-available data about temperatures from the past, you see an even more alarming trend. At the present rate, we shall soon see CO_2 levels higher than Earth has known in millions of years.

The dramatic results of Keeling's measurements got the attention of many more scientists, who began to work on the problem in a variety of creative ways. Some figured out how to determine what temperatures had been in the past by studying tree rings, fossilized corals, and fossilized or frozen grains of pollen. Others began to work on ways to predict what might happen as a result.

Wait, It's Getting Cooler

Meanwhile, something else happened that confused things a bit. The data on historical average temperatures revealed that between the 1940s and the early 1970s, the trend toward warmer temperatures temporarily reversed. Global average temperatures, which had been steadily increasing, began to get cooler rather than warmer. This did not match the rising CO_2 levels, which should have made the planet warmer, not cooler. Some media outlets began reporting the possibility that Earth was entering a new ice age, but few scientists agreed. The effect was localized (mainly in the northern hemisphere), and the local cooling, it seemed, was bringing down the average temperatures. Overall, however, the planet was still trending warmer.

As scientists studied the cooling effect more closely, they learned that it was in part due to an increase during those years of **aerosols** (later banned) and other pollutants that tend to bounce sunlight away from Earth. A 2010 study found another reason for the temporary lull in global warming. An influx of cool water into the northern hemisphere from melting glaciers brought down the surface temperature of the northern oceans. It seems that in the short term, global warming can cause localized cooling. And, of course, the average global temperature doesn't rise smoothly from one year to the next, but rises generally with the occasional plateau or even a year with a slight drop in average temperature. But the average global temperature was clearly trending upward, and at an accelerating pace. In any case, the slight midcentury cooling was soon replaced by a return to rapidly increasing temperatures due to the greenhouse effect.

At this time, climate modeling was still a young science, and little research had been done on the effects of adding so much carbon dioxide to the atmosphere so quickly. The initial data, however, was alarming enough that in 1979, US president Jimmy Carter asked the National Academy of Sciences, a nonprofit, nongovernmental organization of scientists and scholars, to study the issue. The organization convened a nine-member panel, headed by Jule Charney, a meteorologist at the Massachusetts Institute of Technology (MIT). Charney studied, among other things, the feedback patterns between the oceans and the atmosphere, and had pioneered the use of computers and computer modeling to forecast weather patterns. The panel, officially called the Ad Hoc Study Group on Carbon Dioxide and Climate, looked carefully at the work that had been done so far and took pains to check for flaws in models. They didn't find any. The final report of the Charney panel said, "If carbon dioxide continues to increase, the study group finds no reason to doubt that climate changes will result and no reason to believe that these changes will be negligible. The conclusions of prior studies have been generally reaffirmed." They concluded that when the amount of CO_2 in the atmosphere was double what it had been before the Industrial Revolution, the global average temperature would be warmer by about 3°C (5.4°F). That might not seem like much, but think of it like this: at the end of the last ice age, global average temperatures rose about 4 to 7 degrees over a period of five thousand years. That took us from a mostly ice-covered planet to the comfortable

The Carbon Cycle

When you read about climate, you read a lot about carbon. Carbon is the fourth most abundant **element** on Earth. All living things contain carbon. Most of Earth's carbon is stored in rocks—the rest is in the oceans, the atmosphere, the soil, and plants. Carbon is continually exchanged among these storage places in something called the carbon cycle. This storage and exchange system helps keep all the carbon from being in the atmosphere at one time or from all being stored in rocks. This is one of the ways Earth keeps a more or less stable climate.

In the atmosphere, carbon combines with oxygen (another element) to form carbon dioxide—CO_2. (That means one molecule of carbon and two of oxygen.) Plants suck this CO_2 out of the atmosphere and use it to make food. That's one reason that plants and trees—like the rain forest—are important in slowing down global warming. When plants die, they turn into fossil fuels, like coal and oil. Then humans come along and burn them, putting some of that carbon dioxide back into the air. Then new plants suck it back out of the air. The oceans absorb a lot of carbon as well. However, as we have seen, in modern times, humans are burning so much fossil fuel and putting so much carbon dioxide into the atmosphere—and cutting down so many forests that would help absorb it—that carbon is building up in the atmosphere too quickly to keep global temperatures at safe levels.

climate we enjoy today. At the present rate of global warming, we can expect to see that much change in less than a century (we're already halfway there). Fiercer and more frequent storms, more and longer droughts in some areas, flooding of coastal areas as sea levels rise, difficulty growing crops, and the loss of many species of plants and animals as their habitats change are just a few of the expected results of the climate change path Earth is on now. So while a couple of degrees doesn't seem like much, such a small amount of change can mean the difference between a planet that can sustain human life and one that can't.

The Models Are Working

In the decades since the Charney report, hundreds more studies have been done to verify these conclusions and to study in greater depth the relationship between CO_2 and climate. Ice cores drilled from the ice sheet in Greenland have shown that at times in the past, temperatures changed not over the course of centuries, but within decades, something climatologists call "abrupt climate change events." It turns out that Earth's climate is a very delicate system. Small changes can have big consequences. Many different factors can influence the system, and can even tip it very rapidly in one direction or another. As more people worked on the problem, computer models improved. However, at this stage modeling was still somewhat primitive; modelers had to make assumptions about some of the data they input, which made the results somewhat questionable. It was clear that we needed to know a great deal more about the interrelationships in various ecosystems, and how those factors interact with climate and atmosphere, before the models could be reliable. Fortunately, the initial data coming out and the conclusions of the Charney report were so convincing that governments and universities were willing to provide more funding to climate researchers. One thing they learned was that carbon dioxide, while the most significant of the greenhouse gases, was not the only one causing trouble. The amount of **methane** and **chlorofluorocarbons** in the atmosphere was also increasing dramatically. Humans were putting even more gases in the air that were likely to increase global warming. What had looked like a problem we had decades to solve was becoming more and more urgent. Fortunately, climate modeling was soon to get even more accurate.

James Hansen was a physicist who began his scientific career studying the atmosphere on Venus. However, when he learned of the increase in Earth's greenhouse gases, he turned his attention to the atmosphere of his home planet. By 1979, Hansen had developed a climate model that accurately predicted most of what has happened to the climate since. In 1988, a US Senate committee held a hearing on the subject, and Hansen, then director of NASA's Institute for Space Studies, was called to testify. He told the committee that "global warming has reached a level such that we can ascribe with a high degree of confidence a cause-and-effect relationship between the greenhouse effect and observed warming … It is already happening now."

That same summer, in Toronto, Canada, at the World Conference on the Changing Atmosphere, an international group of scientists called on world leaders to enact policies to limit emissions of greenhouse gases. The Toronto group issued a statement that read in part, "humanity is conducting an unintended, uncontrolled, globally pervasive experiment whose ultimate consequences could be second only to a global nuclear war."

Now even more scientists began to do climate change research, and the data became even more convincing. One alternative explanation for the global temperature increase that

One early contemporary explanation for global warming was an increase in solar activity.

had been popular among some was that it was due to an increase in the sun's activity. For some years, sun activity had increased along with global temperatures—even though nobody could come up with a good reason for how that might work. However, in the 1990s, solar activity dropped significantly, while global temperatures continued to soar, making it even less likely that solar activity was the primary cause of warming. Then, a few years later, an analysis of millions of measurements in all of the world's oceans determined that the long-term pattern of warming matched the computer predictions of a greenhouse effect signature. As researchers got more observational and laboratory data to use in their climate models (and no longer had to make assumptions about some of the data), the pattern not only held, but the models accurately described past climates as well—ice ages past. If computer models were able to accurately "predict" what had happened in the past, there was good reason to have confidence in their ability to forecast the future. The models were also good at predicting climate responses to things like volcanic eruptions (Hansen correctly modeled the climate effects of the 1991 eruption of Mount Pinatubo in the Philippines), further boosting confidence in their predictions.

By the end of the twentieth century, it was clear that the planet was getting warmer—fast. Evidence was mounting that the primary driver of the increase in temperature was an accumulation of CO_2 in the atmosphere, caused by the burning of fossil fuels. However, climate is a very complex system, and there was a great deal more work to do to understand exactly what was happening, what the results would be, and what was the best thing to do about it.

2

The Twenty-First Century: From Measurements to Predictions

The twenty-first century arrived—the century in which temperatures were expected to reach dangerous levels if nothing was done to limit the amount of CO_2 being put in the atmosphere. In 1957, when Charles David Keeling began taking his measurements, it seemed like we had a lot of time to fully understand and deal with the problem. But as exploding fireworks and popping champagne corks heralded the beginning of a new century, those who were aware of what was happening to Earth's climate saw the milestone as something more sinister. Not only was the climate change clock ticking, it was ticking faster and faster.

The IPCC Weighs In

Back in 1988, the United Nations Environment Programme (UNEP) and the World Meteorological Organization (WMO)

Opposite: The Greenland ice sheet, the largest ice sheet outside of Antarctica, is rapidly melting, which could cause a dangerous rise in sea levels.

had set up the Intergovernmental Panel on Climate Change (IPCC). The IPCC is an independent, international group of scientists and other experts—thousands of experts from over one hundred nations—who volunteer their time to evaluate and explain the science on climate change to policymakers in the UN member governments, giving them reliable information on which to base their policies. Because it is made up of many scientists, from many different fields, and with various approaches to the problem and few obligations to anything other than the science, the IPCC is widely respected by governments and scientists worldwide.

In 1990, the group began issuing periodic reports assessing the current state of the science on climate change and the socioeconomic effects of a warming Earth. Science is slow and painstaking work, and scientists are naturally cautious people. Though it was already abundantly clear that Earth was rapidly warming and that human activities were contributing to this warming, the details about how soon the effects would be felt, exactly how much of the change was due to the burning of fossil fuels and how much to other factors, what the long-term effects would likely be, and what was the best course of action to prevent disaster were all still matters of research. It took several years before the IPCC produced a report that reflected a **consensus** of representatives from all the nations involved.

In 2001, the IPCC issued its Third Assessment Report (TAR). While couched in very cautious language—particularly with regards to the socioeconomic aspects of climate change—the findings were stark. TAR concluded that the evidence supporting global temperature increases over the next century was even greater than had been previously suggested. The report also stated that the evidence of climate change being due in large part to human activity was strong and getting stronger. The report noted that the factors causing climate change could create something like a feedback loop, with one cause reinforcing another, thereby further accelerating the increase in temperatures. "Changes in vegetation, through either direct **anthropogenic** deforestation or those caused by global warming," the panel wrote, "could occur rapidly *and could induce further climate change.*" [Italics added] They then cited the rapid creation of the Sahara Desert, more than five thousand years ago, as an example of how this kind of extreme change can occur. This report basically confirmed that scientists had ample information to say with confidence that the climate was more likely than not to change during the coming century, and they were able to make some predictions about what the impacts of that change might be. The science of global warming was solid. The choice about whether or not to intervene was up to the world's governments.

The Future Is Here

Over the next few years, the findings of the IPCC's Third Assessment Report were reviewed and affirmed by virtually all of the world's scientific organizations, including the science academies of every one of the world's major nations. Meanwhile, scientists continued to work on the details, improving models and more closely examining potential impacts. In 2007, the IPCC issued its Fourth Assessment Report. This time, the report was even starker. It stated that it is "unequivocal" that the climate is warming—there were absolutely no doubts about the science. How hot it would get, the report declared, depended on future levels of heat-trapping emissions (such as CO_2 and other greenhouse gases). If immediate reductions in emissions were made, Earth would still suffer some impacts of global warming because greenhouse gases can remain in the atmosphere for decades or more, but there was still time to stave off the worst impacts. If nothing was done, the report stated, there would be twice as much warming over the next two decades as there would have been if we had stabilized emissions of heat-trapping gases and pollutants at their year-2000 levels.

Scientists all over the world began collecting data, not only to more fully understand what was causing global warming but to analyze and measure its impacts. As the science of climate change has grown, experts from many fields have begun to contribute to the research. Geologists, oceanographers, paleontologists, biologists, botanists, physicists, mathematicians, statisticians, computer scientists, and even economists are now offering their special expertise to the task of figuring out what to expect from the changing climate and how to slow down the warming before it is too late.

fact!

Weather patterns are changing so dramatically and so rapidly that, according to Canada's Earth Sciences Sector, indigenous people in the Arctic are no longer able to predict the weather using the traditional methods of their ancestors.

By 2010, the end of the first decade of the twenty-first century, it was clear that the climate was warming dangerously fast. It was also increasingly clear that the change was due to human activity. Soon, the consequences of that warming began to appear—even earlier than the more conservative estimates had predicted. The measurements taken in the first decade of the twentieth century showed not only

Scientists remove a core of ice from an Antarctic ice sheet. The air trapped there will show them what the atmosphere was like when the ice froze, many years ago.

that global warming was well under way but that the effects of it were under way as well.

Though we have been talking about global averages, the warming is not uniform around the planet. It is far more pronounced the closer you get to the poles. Temperatures throughout Canada have been increasing at roughly double the global mean rate. The Arctic is warming even faster than that. Because the effects of global warming are likely to impact regions closer to the poles sooner and more forcefully than in other places, much useful data is being gathered from Canada. Earth Sciences Sector (ESS), a part of National Resources Canada, makes systematic, long-term measurements of several indicators of climate change. They measure permafrost, glacier mass balance, and snow cover. Remote sensing provides information about lake and river ice, land cover, and what kind and how much vegetation is growing. They monitor changes in the nation's coastline both by satellite images and field investigations. In the United States, the Environmental Protection Agency and NASA (the National Aeronautics and Space Administration), along with other agencies, have been tracking the effects of climate change using data from dozens of scientific organizations, universities, and research institutions. Elsewhere, the United Nations Environmental Program, the European Environment Agency, and the World Meteorological Organization are all tracking impacts of climate change. The results are sobering.

Since the late nineteenth century, global average temperatures have risen about 2°F (1.1°C), but most of that increase has come in the past thirty-five years. According to NASA, the year 2016 was the hottest on record, and eight of the twelve months of that year were the hottest on record for that month (January through

September, with the exception of June). Both days and nights are becoming hotter, on average, with less cooling off at night.

Much of this heat is being absorbed by the oceans. Ocean temperature has increased considerably in recent years. The top 700 feet (213 meters) has warmed about 0.3 degrees in the last half-century. This may not seem like much, but it has a significant effect on marine ecosystems. Already, many sea animals are suffering from the warmer water temperatures. Krill, which are small animals that live in the ocean and feed on plankton, are a primary food source for many ocean animals, such as whales, seals, and birds. Krill breed in the very cold water near sea ice. When there is less very cold water, there are fewer places for krill to breed. As the oceans have warmed, krill populations have dropped by more than 80 percent. The loss of this tiny animal at the bottom of the food chain could cause the ocean's entire food web to unravel. Without krill, most of the animals in the Antarctic would perish.

Animals that live in warmer parts of the sea are also being affected and are shifting their habitats to adjust to changing water temperatures. Between 1982 and 2015, 105 species of ocean fish and invertebrates have moved about 10 miles (16 kilometers) north and an average of 20 feet (6 m) deeper than their traditional habitats. Shellfish have shifted even further—some by as much as 100 miles (161 km).

Corals are also suffering because of warmer ocean temperatures. Corals are very delicate animals. They live in shallow water and build elaborate skeletons (coral reefs) around themselves. Some types of algae live on the corals—using the corals for protection and in turn providing food for the corals. Algae make food by photosynthesis, using the sunlight that filters

Coral reefs, some of the most diverse habitats on Earth, are being severely damaged by increasing seawater temperatures.

through in the shallow water. Many fish and other sea animals live in and around coral reefs, eating the algae and hiding from predators. However, when the water becomes too warm, the algae cannot make food, the algae die, and then the corals become weak and eventually die as well. This is called coral bleaching, and much like the situation with the krill, it can cause the collapse of entire ecosystems.

Warming oceans are also causing the Greenland and Antarctic ice sheets to shrink. Between 2002 and 2006, Greenland lost between 36 and 60 cubic miles (150 to 250 cubic kilometers) of ice sheets. Antarctica lost about 36 cubic miles (150 cubic km) in roughly the same period—and the shrinking hasn't slowed since then. Satellite images show that in just the four years from 2011 to 2014, Greenland lost 1 trillion tons (907 trillion metric tons) of ice. Arctic sea ice has also declined in both extent and thickness in recent years. In the summer of 2017, the break off of a large section of Antarctica's Larsen C ice shelf was widely covered, a dramatic reminder of the problem.

The melting of polar ice sheets and glaciers is causing sea levels to rise. The global sea level rose about 8 inches (20 centimeters) in the last century, and the rate of the rise is rapidly increasing as well—nearly doubling in the last two decades. Rising sea levels will have a wide range of consequences, including coastal erosion; higher storm surges that reach further inland, destroying homes and infrastructure; coastal communities that are completely and permanently submerged in water; and saltwater penetrating the groundwater, resulting in less fresh water for drinking and agriculture. Rising sea levels have already caused loss of land along some coasts. Satellite imagery of the Atlantic coast of the United States shows significant loss of coastal land on the Southeast coast and somewhat less, but still a large amount, along the mid-Atlantic coast. Fish have been swimming in the streets of South Florida cities on sunny days during high tide.

As more carbon dioxide is being put into the air and then absorbed by the oceans, the oceans are also becoming more acidic. Samples have shown that the acidity of the surface waters of the world's oceans has increased by almost one-third. In some ways, it is a good thing that the ocean absorbs a great deal of the CO_2 humans pump into the air—it slows down the increase of greenhouse gases in the atmosphere. But that benefit comes at great cost. Increased ocean acidification has a detrimental effect not only on corals but also on other sea life, such as oysters, clams, and certain types of plankton. Damaging these life forms can create an effect that ripples throughout the entire ocean food web—including seafood that humans eat and make their livings catching, processing, and selling. Much of the potential damage is still unknown; scientists are currently studying the effects of ocean acidification.

Warming ocean temperatures have an effect on the planet's climate even on land. One of the main jobs of the ocean is to redistribute heat around the planet. Operating somewhat like a giant conveyor belt, ocean currents carry warm surface water to the poles and cold deep water back toward the equator. This warmer surface water helps keep countries in the northern part of the northern hemisphere from being too cold. When melting glaciers add more cold, fresh water to the mix, it can potentially disrupt this flow. Cold salt water is denser than warm water, and so it sinks toward the bottom. But if too much fresh water—from melting glaciers, for example—floods into the ocean, the water becomes less salty and therefore less dense, keeping it from sinking, thereby disrupting the circulation that powers the "conveyor belt." Recent research has shown that this is already starting to happen. It will be a very long time before there is enough change in the circulation to send Northern Europe into an ice age, but devastating results could come long before that. Warm water takes up more area than cold, so this could cause rising sea levels on the east coast of North America, potentially flooding cities like Boston and New York, and possibly inundating Canada's Prince Edward Island, parts of Nova Scotia, and Newfoundland.

It's not just ocean water that is warming. Stream temperatures in some areas have increased in recent years. For example, between 1960 and 2015, the temperature of the water in the Snake River in eastern Washington State increased by 1.4 degrees Fahrenheit (0.7°C), potentially affecting the salmon who use the Snake River to migrate and spawn. These fish are an important part of the diet, culture, and economy of the area.

Birds are shifting their ranges and altering their migration patterns as well. North American birds have moved their wintering grounds on average 40 miles (64 km) northward since 1966. Some have moved hundreds of miles north. Trees and flowers are blooming at different times of year. When plants bloom earlier than in the past, it can have a domino effect on other species. For example, the red knot is a species of shorebird that nests in the Arctic in northern Russia and spends winters on the coast of West Africa. The snow in the little bird's breeding grounds now melts two weeks earlier than it did a few decades ago. This early spring causes the plants there to bloom earlier, which means that

A Disappearing Home

The impacts of climate change will likely affect everyone on Earth at some point, in ways either small or large. But some communities are experiencing the effects sooner than others— and in harsher ways.

Lennox Island is a small First Nations community off Prince Edward Island, Canada. The rhythm of life on Lennox Island is, like most coastal communities, very much tied to the rhythms of the sea. In recent years, those rhythms have been changing. Storms are stronger and more frequent. Summers are warmer and winters milder. Most troubling is the sea level rise. "We're losing our island," one citizen told a reporter from the *Guardian*, a British newspaper. In 1880, the island had 1,520 acres (615 hectares) of land. In 2015, the island had only 1,100 acres (445 ha). Three football fields' worth of land have been, as the article in the *Guardian* put it, "swallowed by the sea." The bridge to the mainland is in danger, as is the water supply to the island.

Sadly, many of the people most immediately and directly affected by climate change are, like the First Nations people of Lennox Island, the ones who have contributed the least to the problem.

Opposite: The Native communities on Lennox Island are being directly affected by the changing climate.

Longer and more severe droughts are among the more obvious, and devastating, impacts of global warming.

the insects that feed on the plants emerge earlier as well. Red knots, which eat the insects, don't hatch in time to feed on the insects while the food source is at its peak. As a result, red knots now have smaller bodies and shorter bills. This makes it difficult for them to dig into the sand to retrieve clams and mussels when they get to Africa for the winter. This is just one of many examples of how sudden changes in hatching seasons and habitats can have far-reaching—and often unanticipated—consequences for a wide range of interconnected species. We not only share Earth with many other species, we all depend on each other, and in ways we don't always appreciate until something starts to go wrong.

Extreme Weather Ahead

Global average temperatures have been setting records in the first part of the new century, but local records are being broken as well. Extreme weather events are on the rise. Not all of these can be pinned on human-caused climate change, but many certainly can—and evidence is growing for others. There is strong evidence that longer and more frequent droughts, and increased rain and snowfall in some areas, are due to global warming. Despite some local record snowfalls, satellite images have shown that the snow cover in the northern hemisphere has decreased in the past few decades, the depth of snowpack has decreased, and the snow is melting earlier. Total snowfall has decreased in the United States in recent years because warmer winters and early springs bring more rain and less snow.

Total **precipitation** has increased worldwide. However, that increase has not been uniform. Some areas, such as the southwest United States, have received far less precipitation than normal, resulting in droughts, while other areas are experiencing more frequent flooding. Warmer air holds more moisture, thus increasing rainfall in some areas that are experiencing warmer temperatures. However, higher temperatures also cause increased evaporation through plant leaves and surface soil. In some areas, even where there is a normal amount of precipitation, increased surface evaporation can make the soil dry out much faster than it normally would. When this happens, more of the sun's heat goes into heating soil and the surrounding air instead of evaporating moisture. This makes summers hotter in these places. In 2011, many locations in Texas and Oklahoma saw more than one hundred days when the temperature was over 100°F (37°C). Both states set records for the hottest summer since 1895, when this kind of recordkeeping began. Rates of water loss through evaporation were double the long-term average. The excessive heat and drought that summer contributed to losses of more than ten billion dollars just in agriculture in these two states.

According to the 2014 US Climate Assessment Report, the incidence of extreme single-day precipitation events has increased dramatically since the 1980s. In the United States, nine of the top ten years for extreme precipitation events have occurred since 1990. The amount of rain falling in very heavy precipitation events in the Northeast, Midwest, and upper Great Plains of the United States has increased more than 30 percent above the 1901–1960 average.

Tropical storms in the Atlantic Ocean, the Caribbean, and the Gulf of Mexico have increased in intensity and frequency during the last twenty years. (Warmer surface temperatures of ocean waters contribute to more frequent and more severe tropical storms.) Changes in methods of studying tropical storms make it difficult to track the changes in the intensity of storms over a long period of time, but this is an indicator worth watching.

A changing climate can produce different weather patterns, causing allergies to be more severe than usual.

Today, weather patterns are becoming hard to predict and weather events are becoming more severe.

Weather versus Climate

While many impacts of global warming are already being seen, such as melting glaciers and changing migration patterns, it can be misleading to look at local weather to get an impression of how the global climate is changing. This is because we sometimes confuse weather with climate. Weather is what's happening in the atmosphere over a short period of time. (For example: Did it snow a lot this winter? Is it raining outside right now?) Climate is patterns of the atmosphere over long periods of time. Scientists who study climate change are looking at the daily averages—for the entire planet—over many, many years. This gives an accurate picture of what's going on with the climate but may not have much to say about what is happening outside right now.

Because weather is so chaotic, it can be hard for weather forecasters to determine what the weather is going to be like more than a few days ahead—and sometimes even today. But since climate is the study of long-range patterns and averages, it's much easier to make predictions. It seems odd, but it is actually easier to predict what the climate will be like two decades from now that it is to predict what the weather will be like next week.

Growing seasons are changing as well, and traditional patterns of what crops can be grown in what areas are shifting. In most US states, especially in the West, the growing season has lengthened, though in some southeastern states, it has shortened, due to spring arriving earlier, bringing hotter weather sooner, and fall arriving later, pushing the first frost date to later in the season. While this may seem like a good thing—more warm weather, more time to grow food—that is not always the case. Many crops require cooler temperatures to **germinate**, and many types of plants—such as some fruit trees—require a certain number of days below freezing in order to bloom and bear fruit later in the year.

Wildfires can be beneficial, but the frequency of wildfires has increased since the 1980s, and so has the fires' severity. According to data from the National Interagency Fire Center, the increase in wildfires corresponds with the increase in temperatures. Of the ten years with the largest amount of land burned, nine have been since 2000. The warmest years on record have also been during this period.

People, Too

Humans are being directly affected by climate change as well. Because so many factors are involved (such as age and underlying health issues), it can be hard to analyze the patterns, but deaths from heat-related illnesses have been increasing in the United States since 1979. Warmer temperatures and later fall frosts have increased the amount of time that trees and other plants release pollen, prolonging allergy season. Since 1995, the length of the ragweed pollen season has increased in ten of eleven sites studied in Canada and the United States. Longer warm seasons increase the number of insects. Incidents of Lyme disease, an illness caused by a bacterial infection spread by ticks, have increased in recent years, and the distribution of cases has spread over a larger geographical area. Mosquito-borne illnesses, such as West Nile virus, are also increasing as late frosts and early springs contribute to greater mosquito populations. Rising ocean temperatures can result in more bacteria and more frequent blooms of harmful algae, and in new locations. Humans can be exposed to bacteria and algae toxins by eating contaminated seafood, drinking contaminated water, or swimming in infested water. These toxins can cause serious illness and in some cases death. Elderly people, children, pregnant women, and people with chronic illnesses are all vulnerable to the health effects of an increasingly warm climate.

These are just a few of the indicators of climate change—that is, observations and calculations that track conditions and trends—that scientists around the world are watching. Monitoring these conditions and trends helps scientists, governments, and businesses assess the effects and potential effects of climate change so that they can make informed decisions about the best way to prevent the worst consequences of a warming planet. As the evidence for human-caused climate change has mounted and the effects have started to show up, governments, businesses, and ordinary citizens have begun to respond in ways large and small.

3

The World Reacts

T housands of people are crowded onto the green of a college campus on a lovely spring day in 1970. A band is playing rock music in the amphitheater, and across the green on the steps of the library, a biology professor is giving a lecture about how pesticides can accumulate in soils. Barefoot hippies wearing tie-dyed T-shirts and neatly groomed businesspeople in suits and skirts crowd in to listen. A little girl is wearing a T-shirt that says, "Let me grow up." A woman is holding a sign warning, "Caution: Use of Standard Oil Products is Hazardous to Your Health." Several people are wearing gas masks to protest air pollution. Signs are everywhere: *Flower Power. Eat Sleep Recycle. Don't Be Fuelish. Good Planets are Hard to Find. Love Your Mother* (under a picture of Earth).

Teach-Ins and Marches

At this point, the science of global warming was still very new, the evidence that human activities were a main driver of climate

Opposite: Bicyclists gather in Colorado on Earth Day 1970 to demand better environmental policies.

change was still weak, and very few people outside the scientific community were aware of global warming. Even scientists had not yet accumulated enough evidence to convince them that human actions were one of the main drivers of the increasing temperatures. However, people did know that the increasing use of pesticides, frequent oil spills, factories dumping pollution into the air and water, the increasing loss of wilderness, and the extinction of many species of animals and plants were dangerous to human health and the health of Earth's ecosystems. The public was becoming increasingly alarmed about the state of the environment—even though most politicians were not.

One exception was a US senator from Wisconsin, Gaylord Nelson. In the late 1960s, Senator Nelson began traveling around the country, talking to people about the state of the environment. While on a tour in the summer of 1969, Nelson noticed that demonstrations against the Vietnam War, which was in full throttle at this time, were spreading rapidly on college campuses. These were often organized as "teach-ins," an idea pioneered at the University of Michigan that combined public education and nonviolent protest. Professors and others knowledgeable about the matter would hold seminars, rallies, and give speeches that informed students and the public of the many issues surrounding the war.

Nelson realized that it was a perfect format for an environmental movement. He thought that if he could tap into the student energy that was powering the antiwar demonstrations, he could organize a huge grassroots movement to spread the news about what was happening to the environment and demand changes from the nation's leaders. He began planning and promoting a nationwide environmental teach-in to take place in April 1970. The idea took off, and organizers from all across the country pitched in.

On April 22, 1970, more than twenty million people gathered in city parks, town squares, and on college campuses across the nation to speak up for the planet. It was the first Earth Day, an event that marked the beginning of the environmental movement. Two thousand colleges and universities and ten thousand primary and secondary schools held teach-ins to bring awareness about the environment and demand that it be protected. It was the largest organized demonstration in American history. Newscaster Walter Cronkite described it as "a day dedicated to enlisting all the citizens in a bountiful country in a common cause of saving life from the deadly by-products of that bounty." The first Canadian Earth Day, Earth Day Canada, was held in 1980. By 1990, the event was global.

fact!

In 2007, the IPCC and Al Gore shared the Nobel Peace Prize for their work verifying and sharing information on climate change.

By the end of the 1980s, as it was becoming increasingly clear that global warming was under way and that humans were causing at least some of it, the emphasis began to shift from bringing about education and awareness of environmental issues to actively trying to change public policy so as to slow down global warming and prevent the worst of its impacts.

Not Just Talking Anymore

Citizens didn't just demonstrate; they organized. In 1971, a small group of antiwar activists in Vancouver, Canada, formed an organization called Greenpeace. The initial aim of the organization was to bring an end to nuclear testing and create a "green and peaceful world." Soon, however, Greenpeace turned its formidable attention more directly to the environment. Their first action was to sail an old wooden boat into the US nuclear test site at Amchitka Island, off the coast of Alaska. Amchitka was home to a variety of wildlife, including bald eagles, peregrine falcons, and three thousand endangered sea otters. By sailing into the area, Greenpeace hoped to prevent the US military from testing a nuclear bomb. Their boat was intercepted before it reached the island, and the bomb was detonated anyway. However, the stunt gained a great deal of publicity. Later that year, the United States stopped testing at Amchitka, and the area was eventually designated a bird sanctuary.

Greenpeace's methods derive from the philosophy of nonviolent protest and peaceful **civil disobedience** taught by Mahatma Gandhi, Martin Luther King Jr., and others. Peaceful they may be, but timid they are not. Greenpeace often uses spectacular tactics to defend the environment and its inhabitants, specializing in issues that affect the oceans or marine environments. In the summer of 1972, the group sailed a yacht donated by a Canadian businessman into the waters near Moruroa in the South Pacific, where the French government was conducting nuclear testing. They hoped to disrupt the tests. A French warship collided with Greenpeace's vessel, bringing international attention to nuclear testing and the group's opposition to it. They used similar tactics in anti-whaling campaigns, confronting whaling vessels in inflatable boats with outboard motors and sparking incidents that brought international attention to this cause. Greenpeace launched campaigns against toxic waste dumping and killing seals for fur. By the early 1980s, their activities were bearing fruit. The European Union banned seal hunting, and the International Whaling Commission vastly limited whale hunting. Limits on toxic waste dumping were enacted by some

The original *Greenpeace* vessel was a creaky old fishing boat, operated by a few dedicated scientists and environmentalists.

nations. Their successes inspired donations, allowing them to buy larger and more well-equipped vessels to wage bigger campaigns.

Things haven't always gone smoothly for the peaceful ecowarriors, however. In 1985, Greenpeace's 417-ton (378 metric-ton) research ship, the *Rainbow Warrior*, was sunk, and one crew member died, when French secret agents placed underwater mines to blow up the ship. (The French government apologized and paid Greenpeace $7 million in settlement, but no one was ever held responsible, and the nuclear testing continued until 1996.) Greenpeace carried on, however, and won many more battles. In recent years, Greenpeace has taken up the cause of global warming. In addition to working to protect the oceans—and particularly the Arctic—the organization is active in the movement to reduce the use of fossil fuels, reduce deforestation, and increase the use of renewable energy.

Not all groups were—or are—as dramatic as Greenpeace. Some take a quieter and more diplomatic approach. The Sierra Club was founded in 1892 by naturalist John Muir. Its early members were mostly scientists who enjoyed exploring the Sierra Nevada Mountains. The group expanded in the twentieth century, but its mission was largely the promotion of enjoyment and stewardship of the outdoors—not political or social change. However, as the warnings about the potential impacts of climate change became more serious and more solidly supported by science, the organization's leaders began to support more action on the issue, including civil disobedience. In 2014, several Sierra Club leaders were arrested—along with dozens of other protestors—when they protested the Keystone XL pipeline, a project to connect the oil sands of Alberta, Canada, with the oil refineries of the US Gulf of Mexico, carrying up to 830,000 barrels of oil per day across the continent. A few weeks later, the Sierra Club filed a lawsuit against the Army Corps of Engineers, demanding the government make public the documents related to its review of the project. In addition to the possibilities of oil spills along the pipeline, the project would, said its opponents, exacerbate global warming, by, among other things, committing the world to the most carbon-intensive source of energy on the planet and committing Canada to developing its oil fields at the expense of investing in sustainable energy sources.

When US president Barack Obama was considering whether or not to approve the project, the US Environmental Protection Agency (EPA) advised against the plan. In addition to its potential harms, it would not, according to the EPA, lower gas prices, create a significant number of long-term jobs, or make a big difference in the United States' energy independence from the Middle East. Obama decided to withhold approval for the project. However, his successor, Donald Trump, issued the required permits within days of taking office in 2017, and a few months later, he formally approved the project. The response from environmental groups was immediate and fierce. The climate activist group 350.org, formed in 2008 by journalist and climate activist Bill McKibben, was at the head of resistance to Keystone XL. However, many other environmental and climate groups were united to oppose the project.

In the case of Keystone XL—as well as many other climate issues—the face of the battle was on the streets, during marches and protests, but the work was being done behind the scenes in statehouses, congressional offices, and in the courts. Environmental activists sued the US State Department, alleging that they did not follow proper administrative procedure and US law for reauthorizing the plan, possibly violating the National Environmental Policy Act. Meanwhile, over one hundred people filed lawsuits challenging the proposed routes of the pipeline. In addition, protestors boycotted and otherwise discredited the banks that provided financial support for the pipeline. All of these tactics were meant to slow down and frustrate the project, if it couldn't be stopped altogether by government action, and eventually make it not worth the cost or effort. Many, many other groups, such as the Natural Resources Defense Council and the Union of Concerned Scientists, worked on a variety of fronts, from educating the public to lobbying Congress to bringing court challenges, in order to slow down global warming and its impacts.

The Movement Grows Up—and Reaches Out

At the time of the first Earth Day, the environmental movement was mostly young, white, and relatively affluent. In recent years, particularly as the impacts of global warming have begun to manifest, it has become clear that the poorest communities suffer disproportionately from the effects of environmental damage. Low-income communities, communities of color, and communities of recent immigrants are hardest hit by environmental hazards and the effects of climate change. These people are much more likely to live near industrial zones, rail yards, freeways, and toxic waste facilities. The increasing impact of a warming planet also affects the poor and people of color more directly and severely. Many of the people who are losing or likely to soon lose their homes to rising sea levels live in poor island nations, such as the Seychelles and Trinidad and Tobago. Often, nations and people with the smallest carbon footprints—those least responsible for the causes of climate change—are the ones likely to suffer the most.

People who live in poverty do not have the resources to cope with the disasters small and large caused by climate change.

Rebuilding after storms, paying more for food when droughts have decimated crops, or moving to areas that have been less severely affected, are options that the rich have and the poor do not. Hurricane Katrina is a good example, though by no means the only one. When the Category 5 storm hit New Orleans

in August 2005, the majority of the victims were poor, black, and brown. The elderly were disproportionally affected as well. While the affluent were able to leave the city and travel to higher ground, those with few resources had no alternative but to stay and face the brunt of the storm and the devastation of its immediate and long-term aftermath. When their homes were flooded and destroyed, those with no insurance or cash were unable to rebuild. According to a Gallup poll conducted six weeks after the storm, black and poor people were far more likely than white and affluent people to have feared for their lives, worried about the safety of elderly family members in the path of the storm, been separated from their families, gone without food and/or drinking water for at least a day, and spent at least one night in a shelter.

According to the International Displacement Monitoring Center, between 2008 and 2014, more than twenty-two million people were displaced due to climate- or weather-related disasters. Because of an increase in storms, droughts, and other climate-related disasters, the chance of being displaced by extreme climate or weather events is 60 percent greater than it was in the 1970s. A 2015 report by the World Bank found that climate change could potentially result in one hundred million more people living in poverty by 2030, due to the effects of crop yield losses, natural disasters, and an increase in illnesses due to malnutrition, scarcity of water, and increased malaria-spreading insects.

With these facts in mind, climate activists have joined with groups that work for social and economic justice to help reframe the conversation about climate argument in terms of climate justice. Groups such as the Climate Justice Action Network and the Environmental and Climate Justice Program of the NAACP (the National Association for the Advancement of Colored People) are working with traditional environmental organizations to work toward a socially just response to climate change.

Faces of the Movement

Climate activists are largely unknown to most of the public, working more or less anonymously as individuals even when the causes they champion and organizations they build are quite public. However, educating the public and bringing attention to the issue requires a combination of teaching and public speaking skills—and a knack for entertaining doesn't hurt.

David Suzuki began his career as a **geneticist**, studying the genes of fruit flies. By the late 1960s, he was a scientific superstar, doing research and teaching at the University of British Columbia and being awarded a variety of honors for his work. He is also known as a cool guy. A profile in *Maclean's* magazine described him as "at once hip and geeky." Soon he traded the lab bench for the TV studio. Suzuki discovered that he had a gift for explaining science in a way that nonscientists could understand, and this, combined with his natural charm and warmth, led to a new career presenting science to the public. Since 1979, he has been the host of *The Nature of Things*, Canadian Broadcasting Corporation's long-running, internationally distributed science program. By the mid-1980s, however, he had taken on yet another career. In

David Suzuki combines his scientific experience and expertise with a sense of humor and natural charm to educate the public about climate change.

the early 1980s, he became involved in an effort to protect the Queen Charlotte Islands (now called Haida Gwaii) off the coast of British Columbia from clear-cut logging. That led directly to more involvement in environmental issues. Soon Suzuki was the father and face of Canada's environmental movement. In 1991, he established the David Suzuki Foundation, a nonprofit organization dedicated to promoting environmental causes and education. He is very passionate, and sometimes even angry, about what is happening to the planet. Undoubtedly, many of today's climate activists and much of the public in Canada and the United States understand what is at stake largely because of David Suzuki.

If David Suzuki is hip and geeky, Al Gore is a bit more buttoned-up and polished. Where casual for Suzuki is jeans and sandals, for Gore it means rolled-up shirtsleeves and a loosened tie. Though he is a politician, not a scientist, Gore definitely knows the data on climate change as well as any scientist and better than many. One advantage he has when it comes to advocating for climate change is that he knows the science, but he also knows the political system—both in the United States and the world. He was vice president of the United States for eight years under Bill Clinton, but before that he served in the US Congress for sixteen years, first in the House of Representatives and then in the Senate. In 1989, as a US senator, Gore held hearings on climate change, and in 1992 he wrote his first book, *Earth in the Balance*, a close look at the global environmental crisis. Then he put together a slideshow—in those pre-PowerPoint days, he used three Kodak carousels and three projectors—that outlined the climate crisis as it was then understood. He is still continually updating the slideshow as the science emerges and the data changes.

Al Gore is well versed in the science of climate change, but he is also able to use his long years of political experience to advocate for policy changes.

Small Changes

When threats to the environment became clear, especially the potential impacts of climate change, individuals marched in the streets, and organizations geared up to spread the word and influence government policy. But not all the action was in the streets and the halls of power. People concerned about climate change also took action in private. Ordinary citizens all over the world began to make lifestyle changes—small and large—that would help address the problem of human-caused climate change. They turned down their thermostats, bought energy-efficient appliances and fluorescent light bulbs, turned lights off when they weren't using them, began taking shorter showers, and started eating less meat. They also bought energy-efficient cars, drove fewer miles, joined carpools, or even stopped driving altogether. Many city people traded their cars for bicycles or began taking public transportation.

Some of these may seem like small steps, but in fact, small steps can make a big difference. According to the Union of Concerned Scientists, cars and trucks account for one-fifth of all emissions in the United States, so a lot of people driving a little less each week can make a dent in a major source of greenhouse gases.

And what about "eating less meat"? What does that have to do with climate change? While not as big a factor as fossil fuels, meat production is still a major contributor of greenhouse gases. According to a United Nations report, livestock production is responsible for 18 percent of greenhouse gas emissions, less than the transportation sector. Going vegetarian at least part of the time is not only kind to animals, but kind to the planet.

When it comes to reducing emissions, small things aren't always small. When everyone does a little bit, the effect can be huge.

Gore lost the 2000 US presidential election in a narrow defeat in which he won the popular vote but lost the Electoral College, and then the US Supreme Court handed the election to his opponent by refusing to allow a recount of the contested Florida vote. After this, he withdrew from electoral politics and threw his full energy into spreading the word about climate change. He hit the road with the slideshow, bringing the message to small and large groups around the country. In 2006, the slideshow was made into a book and a film, both called *An Inconvenient Truth*, which spread the word to millions.

In many ways, before *An Inconvenient Truth*, the strong case for human-caused climate change had not reached very far beyond the world of scientists and those already active in the environmental movement. For a generation of Americans, Al Gore is the voice of climate change. Many who never gave much thought to the fate of the planet or the urgency of the crisis— beyond the yearly Earth Day events and an imperative to reduce, reuse, and recycle—began to take climate change seriously after seeing the film. Gore is still on the road with his message. *An Inconvenient Sequel: Truth to Power* was released in 2017.

Politicians Take Note

After the first Earth Day, politicians did notice. In 1970, US president Richard Nixon created the Environmental Protection Agency, and during the rest of his time in office, he signed a great deal of environmental legislation, including the Clean Water Act, the Clean Air Act, and the Endangered Species Act. Though designed to deal with air pollution, the language of the Clean Air Act included mention of pollution's effect on "climate" or "weather." Leaders at the time wanted the EPA to be

The Indonesian president delivers an address to the Global Ministerial Environmental Forum in 2010, urging delegates to take action on climate change.

able to deal with new problems and new science as they emerged. Compared with ending the Vietnam War, protecting the planet from pollution must have seemed easy. And things did seem to go pretty well for the movement for a few years.

In 1979, the First World Climate Conference was held in Geneva, Switzerland. This was the first major global acknowledgement that humans might play some kind of role in climate change. The conference's official report stated, "Carbon dioxide plays a fundamental role in determining the temperature of Earth's atmosphere, and it appears plausible that an increased amount of carbon dioxide in the atmosphere can contribute to global warming." The report did point out that, as of that time, the mechanism was still poorly understood. In 1988, the IPCC was formed.

In 1992, at a huge meeting called Earth Summit held in Rio de Janeiro, Brazil, nearly every nation signed an agreement to stabilize greenhouse gas emissions at levels that would prevent dangerous human-caused interference with the climate system. (Developing nations, such as China and India, that had not contributed to the buildup of CO_2 were not asked to reduce their emissions.) After years of negotiations, a treaty was hammered out to specify the exact targets for each nation and hold them to the agreement. In 1997, the treaty was finalized at a meeting in Kyoto, Japan, and called the Kyoto Protocol. It took effect in 2005. Nearly every nation signed, with one big exception: the United States, which had withdrawn from the agreement in 2001. Canada followed suit ten years later, withdrawing in 2011.

By 2011, many nations and regions, including the European Union, were on target to meet their Kyoto pledges; however, by the time the treaty took effect, global emissions had increased so much that the targets were too low. The United States and China were pumping out enough CO_2 to totally erase the reductions made by the other countries. Nonetheless, Kyoto marked some progress both in reducing emissions and in the realization that something needed to be done on a national policy level.

In December 2015, after years of negotiations, the world made a huge step toward dealing with climate change. At a historic meeting in Paris, France, 196 nations—including the United States—signed the Paris Climate Agreement. The goal of the agreement is to keep the average global temperature below 2°C (1.1°F), and to make efforts to limit temperature increases to 1.5°C (0.8°F). To do this, countries should enforce carbon emission regulations and reduce their carbon footprint, but how they do it is up to them. Countries are required to report their progress, but some aspects of the agreement are nonbinding, such as setting emissions reductions targets.

The Paris Agreement, imperfect as it is, is undoubtedly the best thing to happen on the global warming front since Guy Callendar noticed that it was happening. Despite this progress, the road has been bumpy for the effort to reduce global warming. From people who deliberately confuse, muddy, and simply deny the science, to politicians who listen to industry **lobbyists** instead of scientists, getting the message out about climate change isn't easy. One particularly difficult blow to the agreement came in the spring of 2017, when US president Donald Trump announced that the United States was pulling out of the Paris Agreement. Several states and many US cities, however, committed to meeting the reduction targets in the treaty, and climate activists did not give up hope of changing the US policy on climate change.

4

Problems Facing Climate Change Action Today

In 1940, when Hitler was rampaging across Europe, US president Franklin Delano Roosevelt was reelected to an unprecedented third term. In one of his regular addresses to the nation, Roosevelt explained that "the Nazi masters of Germany" were intent on enslaving all the nations of Europe, and that unless they were stopped, they would soon come for the rest of the world. Roosevelt painted a grim picture of what the nation would be like if the United States stood idly by and let Hitler have his way. He described letters he had received as saying things like, "Please, Mr. President, don't frighten us with the facts." Yet he did not pretend things were other than they were, and he called on the people of the United States to take seriously the threat of invasion by Hitler's forces and begin immediate action to prevent it. Meanwhile, Americans saw photographs of the devastation in Europe and read reports in the newspapers and in letters from

Opposite: Children in New York City tend vegetables in a Victory Garden in their schoolyard in June 1944.

friends and relatives overseas. Soon, they realized that Roosevelt was right, and they threw themselves into an unprecedented effort to stop the march of totalitarianism.

Those Americans who did not serve in the military once the US joined the war in Europe in 1941 helped in numerous ways. They rolled bandages, grew Victory Gardens, and cheerfully and proudly endured shortages and the rationing of basics such as meat, sugar, and fuel oil. Much was at stake, and the American public was not only willing but eager to rise to the challenge.

Now, almost eighty years later, the world is facing another crisis. The scientific consensus on climate change is virtually unanimous, and the potential impacts are disastrous. So why is the United States not working with the same determination to stop global warming that it did to fight Hitler? To find the answer to that question, we need to go back and take a look at the debate about the risks of smoking tobacco.

Doubt Is Their Product

In 2015, a US district judge ordered the nation's biggest manufacturers of cigarettes to pay for an advertising campaign containing the statement, "A federal court has ruled that the defendant tobacco companies [Altria, R.J. Reynolds Tobacco, Lorillard, and Philip Morris USA] deliberately deceived the American public about the health effects of smoking." (The language was later changed somewhat, and the tobacco companies are still appealing, claiming that the notice amounts to a "forced public confession.") The ruling was based on thousands of court findings that these companies engaged in a willful and organized campaign of fraud designed to deceive the American public and discredit the science that clearly proved the health risks of smoking tobacco.

For many years, ExxonMobil funded climate change denial groups, even as their own scientists uncovered the facts of global warming.

Even though the science on the dangers of smoking had been clear—and widely accepted—for a long time, the tobacco industry manufactured a "controversy" where there was none. An internal tobacco industry memo that surfaced in court cases read: "Doubt is our product, since it is the best means of competing with the 'body of fact' that exists in the mind of the general public. It is also the means of establishing a controversy." The doubt in the public's mind was sown by the public relations efforts of the tobacco industry. They repeatedly claimed that there was "no proof" of the harms of tobacco, even though decades of research had established that smoking tobacco was a direct cause of lung cancer and **cardiovascular** disease. They used techniques that ranged from funding bogus and industry-sponsored studies and getting them published in journals whose editorial boards were staffed with industry representatives (or starting their own journals to publish them), to flooding the media with misleading and false stories to fuel doubt about the science (that was no longer in any serious doubt by credible scientists).

fact!

Multiple studies in **peer-reviewed** scientific journals show that at least 97 percent of active climate scientists agree that it is extremely likely that global warming trends over the past century are due to human activities.

The sordid story of how the tobacco industry manipulated science and deceived the public is no longer a secret, thanks to whistleblowers who exposed documents proving that it was indeed a carefully planned and executed campaign of

In the 1990s, Minnesota attorney general Hubert Humphrey III brought a lawsuit against the tobacco companies to recoup the money the state had spent on the health problems caused by tobacco use. He won.

disinformation, and court cases that examined the evidence and made it public. Happily, the fact that cigarettes are dangerous is no longer questioned by a significant amount of the public. It is not clear, however, that we've learned much from the experience. The techniques developed and honed by the tobacco companies (and a few new techniques) are still being used to sow doubts about science that might inconvenience industry. And the fossil fuels industry is most certainly being inconvenienced by climate change science.

The Playbook

A study published in 2014 found that between 2003 and 2010, the annual income of ninety-one organizations dedicated to raising doubts about climate science amounted to just over $900 million. These groups used the tobacco industry playbook to try to confuse the public about the science of climate change. Rather than addressing the issue from a reasoned position, they spread false information in an attempt to confuse people who do not have the time or background to carefully study the issue. They do not challenge the science directly, by publishing articles in peer-reviewed journals or presenting their findings and arguments at international scientific conferences. Instead, they go straight to the media with misleading and often baseless claims.

One of their favorite techniques is to hire so-called experts to appear on television, in newspapers, and in magazines, stating that there is controversy about the basic claims of climate science and touting scientific studies that either do not exist or that they are misrepresenting. When you check into the backgrounds of these experts, you find that these people are employed by the organizations whose main goal is to discredit climate science.

They are not independent climate scientists who are dedicated to finding out the facts and understanding the science. If you heard someone from an oil or coal company make the claim that, say, wind power actually increases atmospheric CO_2 (a claim actually made by one of these people), you would probably be suspicious. But when you hear the same claim made by a person identified as "an expert" who works for a seemingly independent organization, often with a reassuring-sounding name, like the Heartland Institute, the Institute for Energy Research, or Americans for Prosperity, you are more likely to take him or her seriously. Average citizens don't have the time or the resources to check out the credentials and the source of funding for every person they see interviewed on television. If they did, they would find that the experts challenging climate change are not independent at all, but are being paid by the very people who have the most to lose by shifting away from fossil fuels.

fact!

According to a 2016 Pew survey, 65 percent of Americans—representing views from all parties—are worried about climate change.

In addition to sowing doubts about science, these climate denial groups often try to intimidate and tarnish the reputations of legitimate scientists and even ordinary citizens who publicly challenge them. They spread lies about them on the internet, misrepresent their findings, tarnish their reputations, and even sometimes threaten them with violence. One scientist who found himself in the crosshairs of these groups received an email that said, "You and your colleagues ... ought to be shot, quartered, and fed to the pigs," and another that said the writer hoped to see on the news that he had committed suicide. His

How Science Works

Many people misunderstand the way science works, and that can be an opportunity for people who would—for whatever reason—want to discredit science. Scientists are very skeptical people, and science is a slow and deliberate enterprise. No scientist worth her lab coat is convinced by a single study or by any evidence that has not been carefully examined and subjected to peer review. During peer review, scientists poke and prod and look for weaknesses, and often send the researcher back to the lab to take another look at things, to be sure he or she gets this exactly right. This is why, except for the simplest of issues, it can take a very long time for science to reach a consensus—as it did with the idea that climate change is being driven by human activities. Even when scientists do have a great deal of evidence, they are always looking for more, and are willing to change their thinking if new evidence calls into question previous conclusions. This does not mean, however, that when it comes to global warming and the role of humans in climate change, the science is not settled. It is. The evidence is overwhelming, and virtually all scientists, in many different fields of expertise, agree on this.

family was also threatened. These are not the tactics of people who have a legitimate scientific disagreement. These are the tactics of bullies.

The goal of these campaigns is not to convince people that human-influenced global warming is not happening—they do not have the data or arguments to do that. What they aim to do is simply confuse people, so that the public no longer trusts what they hear from anyone. Sometimes they just lie. A 2012 press release from the Heartland Institute said, "The claim that there is a 'scientific consensus' that global warming is both man-made and a serious problem is untrue." However, every single one of the many organizations of scientists around the world says that there is indeed a "scientific consensus" about human-caused global warming.

Follow the Money

Any doubts that the fossil fuel industry was hiring these organizations to muddy the waters and confuse the public were put to rest a few years ago, when reporters at *InsideClimate News* uncovered documents showing that Exxon (now ExxonMobil, the world's largest oil company) had not only known about the science on climate change for many years, but they had done some of the science themselves. Back in the late 1970s, when climate change was not on the public radar, Exxon invested millions of dollars in climate research, monitoring CO_2 in the air, building climate models, and studying how much CO_2 could be captured in the oceans—one of the big research questions at the time. Their own scientists warned Exxon executives that there was a scientific consensus on human-caused climate change, and that the most likely way humans were contributing to increasing global temperatures was by the release into the atmosphere of CO_2. Their experts warned that we had only a few years—perhaps less than a decade—to make some difficult decisions about energy strategies. Yet when scientist James Hansen testified before Congress in 1988 that global warming was already under way, Exxon did not respond by sharing the research they had done and working to come up with solutions that could protect their industry as well as the people of the world. Instead they created an organization, Global Climate Coalition, to question the science. (That organization was disbanded in 2002, but Exxon continued funding other groups.) Even as their own scientists were confirming the dangers of climate change, Exxon worked to keep the United States and other countries from agreeing to the Kyoto Protocol. In 2014, the Union for Concerned Scientists unearthed internal communications from fossil fuel companies indicating that they were launching a big communications effort to "sow doubt." By using the techniques of the tobacco companies and creating doubt where there was none, these companies slowed efforts to address the global warming problem, making the environmental problem worse, as well as preventing their own industry from being able to make changes that would help them adapt to the economic challenges of climate change.

Peabody Energy, one of the largest coal mining companies in the world, filed for bankruptcy in April 2016 because it could no longer compete with natural gas, which is much cheaper. Environmental groups had long suspected but been unable to prove that the company was funding climate change denial groups. When the company's finances were made public as a result of the bankruptcy, even environmental groups were astonished at the extent to which Peabody had been funding the climate

Get Your Inoculations

By becoming familiar with the techniques used by those who distort or confuse the issue (either intentionally or not), you can **inoculate** yourself against deception in much the same way you get shots to protect yourself from measles and mumps. For example, in an attempt to create "balance," news programs often feature one climate scientist and one climate-change skeptic. This gives the impression that roughly the same number of experts question climate science as support it. Of course, this is far from the truth. In order to project the correct "balance," a news program or talk show would need to have *ninety-seven* scientists for every three skeptics. Of course, it is not necessary to crowd news programs with people in lab coats once viewers understand how news coverage is distorted in this way.

change denial industry. Among the people in the pay of Peabody Coal were several of the small percentage of scientists (less than 5 percent) who do not agree with this science on human-caused climate change.

Perhaps if Peabody had spent that money and energy diversifying their company and retraining workers, they would have been able to provide many thousands of coal miners with even better paying, safer jobs that would not be at risk today because of the economic challenges of the coal industry. And they would have saved years in the effort to reduce global warming. As Kenneth Kimmel, president of the Union for Concerned Scientists, said in a 2014 article in *Scientific American*, "I have to think if the fossil-fuel companies had been upfront about this and had been part of the solution instead of the problem, we would have made a lot of progress … instead of doubling our greenhouse gas emissions."

In 2007, ExxonMobil announced that it would cease funding climate-skeptic groups as of 2008, though according to some reports, they are still funding climate deniers. In any case, other donors, such as the American Petroleum Institute and Koch Industries, were more than able to pick up the slack. In recent years, companies have been funding these organizations with "dark money," funds that are impossible to trace because they have been channeled through other organizations.

Politics

Confusing and misleading the public was not the only strategy of fossil fuel companies and others opposed to attempts to curb global warming. They spent a great deal of time influencing elected officials as well. As we saw earlier, the Nixon administration was responsive to the demands of the environmental movement, as

US president Jimmy Carter inaugurates the solar panels being installed at the White House roof in 1979.

were the Ford and Carter administrations that followed. US president Jimmy Carter, elected in 1976, introduced and backed environmental legislation, increased the budget of the EPA, and established the US Department of Energy. He also installed solar panels on the White House and famously wore a sweater while addressing the nation from the White House, explaining that he had turned down the thermostats at the White House and encouraging other Americans to do likewise in their own homes. For his pains, he was branded the "doom and gloom" president by his successor, Ronald Reagan.

Claiming that Carter's environmental policies were a "doomsday scenario," Reagan and the Republican Congress reversed most of the advances made by Carter. In one of his first acts as president, Reagan removed the solar panels from the roof of the White House. Prior to this, the environment had not been a partisan issue—Republicans (Teddy Roosevelt, Richard Nixon) and Democrats (Jimmy Carter) alike had been supportive of efforts to protect the environment. At this point, however, these kinds of issues became increasingly politicized. The efforts of climate-change denial groups inflamed this partisan divide.

ExxonMobil lobbyists worked hard to convince Congress not to approve the Kyoto Protocol, arguing that it would be too expensive and put too much of the burden on developed nations. Though the United States was far and away the biggest emitter of CO_2 at the time, developing nations such as India and China were increasing their emissions rapidly. While those opposed to the Kyoto agreement were busily trying to convince the public that global warming was some kind of hoax, there were, in fact, legitimate issues about the treaty that needed discussion. Seeding distrust about the science, however, made it impossible to have these discussions with any integrity.

In 2001, the United States withdrew from the Kyoto Protocol when President George W. Bush declined to send it to the US Senate for ratification. Canada initially signed the accord but didn't make much effort to meet its targets. In 2011, the Canadian government, under then–Prime Minister Stephen Harper, pulled Canada out completely—in part because the world's two largest CO_2 emitters, the United States and (by that time) China, were not participating in the agreement. (They also claimed that the restrictions would hamper job growth.)

The effect of these efforts to confuse or deny legitimate science is that ordinary citizens who want to understand the facts so that they can make good decisions and elect leaders they believe will make good decisions have a hard time finding those facts. Change is difficult, and facing global warming will require change. But there are many different ways of addressing the problem, and plenty of room for exciting new ideas and approaches. When people don't know the truth about the science, when students aren't taught the facts, and an attitude of distrust rather than cooperation and open inquiry prevails, it is difficult if not impossible to have a reasoned debate and come up with solutions on which everyone can agree.

The public is not as easily deceived as the climate denial industry believes, however. While there have been some recent setbacks, there is every reason to have hope about the future of the planet.

5

It's Late, but Not Too Late

Saturday, December 12, 2015, was a good day for the planet. Normally staid diplomats from around the world leapt to their feet and broke out in cheers, embracing one another and shedding tears of joy—and relief. This was the day that nearly all of the world's nations came together in what the British newspaper the *Guardian* called "the world's greatest diplomatic success," agreeing to limit greenhouse gas emissions so as to keep global temperature increases to less than 2°C (3.6°F) above pre-industrial levels.

After several years of no progress, and even a great deal of backsliding on environmental issues, the United States—one of the world's biggest emitters of greenhouse gases—had finally agreed to the Paris Climate Agreement, as had other reluctant nations, such as China. In the second term of the Obama administration, the United States had reaffirmed a willingness

Opposite: Despite a diminished amount of government support, solar energy farms are popping up all around the United States.

US president Barack Obama and UN secretary general Ban Ki-moon shake hands during the ratification of the Paris Climate Agreement in 2016.

to address environmental issues and climate change especially. (President Obama replaced the solar panels on the White House roof—though George W. Bush had already installed a solar electric system in the White House.)

Wait, Hold the Party

However, in June 2017, newly elected US president Donald Trump announced the country would not participate in the Paris Agreement after all. Trump, a long-time climate denier, has called global warming "a hoax" perpetuated by the Chinese in order to make US manufacturing less competitive. Scott Pruitt, appointed head of the EPA in 2017, rejects the international scientific consensus on human-caused global warming. The administration has also removed much of the climate science research from official government websites. In addition, the Trump administration has vowed to roll back the Clean Power Plan, an Obama-administration program that sets flexible state-by-state targets for reducing carbon emissions and investing in clean energy.

Things are troubling in Canada as well. After a decade under a government that was very cozy with the fossil-fuel industry and dealt the nation many environmental setbacks, Justin Trudeau became Canadian prime minister in 2015, promising "real change" on environmental issues. Indeed, he

fact!

According to a report from the International Energy Administration, total global emissions did not increase in 2016. Emissions in Europe, the United States, and China decreased, offsetting increases in other nations.

seemed to move on that promise right away. Canada ratified the Paris Agreement in October 2016. Trudeau, however, has been criticized for not putting forth policies that match his climate-change **rhetoric**. So far his record has been mixed. While he imposed a five-year **moratorium** on oil and gas drilling projects in the Arctic and ended the previous government's **gag order** that prevented government scientists from talking to the media and the public, he has also approved two pipeline projects and supports the Keystone XL Pipeline.

Still Marching

On Earth Day 2017, forty-seven years after the first Earth Day, environmentalists and climate activists teamed up with scientists to march in Washington, DC, with sister marches in more than five hundred other cities. Scientists, though normally very reluctant to get involved in politics, were troubled by the new administration's attempts to silence science (not just on climate change, but on a range of issues), and nonscientists were troubled not only that the Trump administration was reversing years of progress on environmental issues, but that they were actively working to suppress science and keep information from the public. Holding signs saying, "There Is No Planet B," "Make American Smart Again," and "Fight Climate Change or Die Frying" (alongside a picture of a fried egg), protestors demanded both action on climate change and scientific freedom without government interference.

To many, the march—and the need even to have such a march—reflected a low point in the movement to protect the planet and to make sure the public has access to and understands the science of climate change (as well as other science). As a

Bill Nye the Science Guy (wearing a red bowtie), a popular science communicator, joined thousands of scientists and other concerned citizens to march on Washington in April 2017.

sign carried by an older protestor put it, "I can't believe I'm still having to march about this." But to many others, the march was an indication of hope. The very fact that so many people—in the United States and elsewhere—were willing to take to the streets and speak up when the independence of science seemed in jeopardy and the fate of the planet in the balance was encouraging. It turns out that, despite some ominous signs and a rapidly ticking clock, there is a great deal to be optimistic about.

Despite public relations efforts on behalf of the fossil fuels industry, corporate America is becoming increasingly open to clean energy. Most major coal, natural gas, and oil companies either back the Paris Climate Agreement or are not lobbying against it. Rex Tillerson, former CEO of ExxonMobil and US secretary of state, recommended that the United States stay in the agreement, and ExxonMobil sent a letter to Trump asking him to stay in the agreement. (It was under Tillerson's leadership that ExxonMobil announced it would cease funding climate change deniers and publicly acknowledged that "the accumulation of greenhouse gases in Earth's atmosphere poses risks that may prove significant for society and ecosystems.") In an interview in 2017 with a news outlet, the CEO of Cloud Peak Energy, a major US coal company, said, "It seems absolutely irrational to not at least develop an insurance policy against climate change. What if the planet is warming up twice as much as we thought?"

In addition, investors are beginning to realize that dirty energy is a bad long-term investment and are putting their money behind renewables. Ironically, much of the resistance to clean energy policy has been based on the argument that it is bad for the economy (and will cost jobs), but clean energy is likely to win in the end precisely because it is proving to be very good for the economies of the nations that embrace it. According to the United

What Can I Do?

Most of us these days are aware of the problem of human-caused global warming and are taking steps to reduce our impact on the planet. We turn down our thermostats, save water, and hang our clothes out to dry rather then spinning them in the dryer. But sometimes it seems like all these daily efforts aren't helping much. While we are all working to "save the planet," politicians and policymakers are making the decisions that will determine our fate. The people who are in school right now will have to live with the consequences of the decisions. However, you don't have to wait until you are old enough to vote to make your voice heard and influence policy.

If you want to help, the first thing to do is educate yourself. Make sure you understand the problem and the advantages and disadvantages of proposed solutions. Be aware of fake science and attempts to deceive you, but also be open to discussion and the nuances of the issue. Then you'll be ready to advocate for better climate policies by writing letters to your Congressional representatives and meeting with your local politicians. Talk with your parents and other adults in your life to let them know how important this issue is to you. Never for a moment think that just because you are a young person, you can't have an effect on the world. Young people were the driving force behind the movement that helped stop the Vietnam War. And young people now are the best hope for the future of the planet.

Nations, the world's capacity for clean energy is expanding (particularly in Europe), and the cost is coming down rapidly. In 2017, for the first time, the cost of solar and wind energy became lower than the cost of fossil fuels.

As we saw in the last chapter, one of the world's leading coal companies had to file for bankruptcy protection in 2016 not because of increased regulations, but primarily because of competition from cheaper sources of fuel (in this case primarily natural gas). It was one of many coal companies to have gone belly-up recently. But while coal companies are closing mines and laying off workers, renewable energy companies are growing and hiring. The shift to cleaner energy seems to be happening regardless of the rhetoric surrounding it.

Even though the national leadership is waffling on meeting the Paris Agreement, many US cities are setting their own goals. New York, Chicago, Atlanta, Los Angeles, Phoenix—and many others—have set goals that meet or exceed the emissions targets recommended by climate scientists. Other countries, such as European Union nations and China, are already working to meet the goals of the Paris Agreement. Developing nations that earlier resisted being asked to sacrifice their development goals to help fix a problem they had no role in creating are now willing to do what they can. This is in part because they realize that they will bear the brunt of the damage if they do nothing (even if that isn't fair), in part because they've managed to extract some promises of help from developed nations, and in part because developing sustainable energy is looking like a much better economic strategy.

The Road Ahead

While politicians and policymakers are negotiating, making deals, and debating the best way to proceed, scientists are still hard at work, tracking global temperatures and adjusting models and predictions as greenhouse gas emissions and other variables change. Climate science, as we have seen, is an old field, but a somewhat newer branch of study—astrobiology—is asking slightly different questions about humans and our effect on the planet. Astrobiology is the study of life in a planetary context: how life developed on Earth, how it might have developed (and perhaps died out) on other planets, and the potential effects of advanced societies on the ecosystems in which they develop. Why is this important to the study of climate change? It is important because if the people of Earth manage to avert the disaster that is presently confronting us, we can't afford to breathe a sigh of relief and stop paying attention.

One of the biggest mysteries of astronomy is why, with so many planets capable of supporting life, we have not been contacted by a civilization from another planet—and have so far found no evidence of one. There are many possible answers to this question, but one is simply that no civilization that has become advanced enough for interstellar travel or communication has survived long enough to do it. Highly technological civilizations—the kind that can send signals into space—must harvest a tremendous amount of energy, and as we earthlings have learned the hard way, that process is not without cost. Astrobiologists are attempting to figure out what roads we can take that will lead to sustainable

Global warming has had a particular effect on arctic regions, melting ice caps and glaciers at a rapid rate.

human civilizations and prevent our greatest advances from leading to our doom. We must make sure that whatever roads we take in the future—wind power, solar power, or other plans or programs we haven't even dreamed of yet—are carefully studied and understood so that we can never again come this close to annihilating ourselves. And scientists are already working on that.

Meanwhile, many people are asking themselves, "Is it too late? Is there any hope left?" The answer is clear. In the battle against global warming, it is very late—and we have lost a great deal of valuable time arguing about facts that are not truly arguable. However, it is most certainly not *too* late. There is a great deal of reason for hope. If we take this problem seriously, act swiftly, and are willing to make necessary sacrifices and come up with creative solutions, we can stop human-caused global warming before it is too late.

Glossary

aerosol A suspension of fine particles in a gas.

anthropogenic Being caused by humans or human activity.

cardiovascular Having to do with the circulation system, the heart, and/or the blood vessels.

chlorofluorocarbons Gases typically used in refrigerants and aerosol propellants, as well as cleaning solvents and some manufacturing processes.

civil disobedience The nonviolent refusal to obey government demands or rules in an effort to effect changes in policy or society.

consensus General agreement of most of the people concerned with a given issue or situation.

element One of the basic chemical components of matter that cannot be broken down into simpler parts.

exponentially Referring to an extreme or unusually rapid increase.

gag order A court measure taken to prohibit discussion of certain topics.

geneticist A person who studies genes in humans and animals and the phenomenon of inherited traits.

germinate To grow.

inoculate To vaccinate; to attempt to induce immunity to infection-caused illness.

lobbyist Someone who works officially to influence government officials or policy, usually in the pay of an interest group.

methane A colorless, flammable gas that is one of the primary greenhouse gases, often used as a fuel.

moraine A collection of rocks, earth, and other debris deposited by a glacier.

moratorium A temporary stopping or postponing of a practice or policy.

peer review When scientists who are experts in a given area look closely at each others' work to make sure it holds up to scrutiny.

precipitation Rain, snow, sleet, or hail that falls to the ground (as opposed to fog).

rhetoric Language specifically intended to convince or make an argument for a particular position.

Further Information

Books

Bennett, Jeffrey. *A Global Warming Primer: Answering Your Questions About the Science, the Consequences, and the Solutions*. Boulder, CO: Big Kid Science, 2016.

Gore, Al. *An Inconvenient Truth: The Planetary Emergency of Global Warming and What We Can Do About It*. New York: Rodale, 2006.

Hawken, Paul, ed. *Drawdown: The Most Comprehensive Plan Ever Proposed to Reverse Global Warming*. New York: Penguin, 2016.

McKibben, Bill. *The End of Nature*. New York: Random House, 2006.

Nye, Bill. *Unstoppable: Harnessing Science to Change the World*. New York: St. Martin's Press, 2016.

Otto, Shawn. *The War on Science: Who's Waging It, Why It Matters, What We Can Do About It*. Minneapolis, MN: Milkweed Editions, 2016.

Websites

Center for Climate and Energy Solutions

https://www.c2es.org/climatecompass

A project of the Pew Center on Global Climate Change, the CCES is an independent, nonpartisan, nonprofit organization working to forge practical solutions to climate change.

Climate Reality Project

https://www.algore.com/project/the-climate-reality-project

This website explains Al Gore's Climate Reality Project, a nonprofit organization that educates others on climate change.

Real Climate: Climate Science from Climate Scientists

http://www.realclimate.org

This is a site on climate science with commentary and explanation from working climate scientists.

Skeptical Science

https://skepticalscience.com

Skeptical Science is a nonprofit science education organization dedicated to encouraging skepticism and explaining what peer-reviewed science has to say about global warming.

Organizations

Alliance for Climate Education
4696 Broadway
Suite 2
Boulder, CO 80304
https://acespace.org

The Alliance for Climate Education is an organization that educates students about climate change and empowers them to lead on climate solutions.

David Suzuki Foundation
219-2211 West 4th Ave.
Vancouver, BC V6K 4S2
http://www.davidsuzuki.org

The David Suzuki Foundation is an organization that collaborates with Canadian people, government, and businesses to preserve the environment and create a sustainable Canada.

350
20 Jay Street
Suite 732
Brooklyn, NY 11201
https://350.org

350 is a nonprofit organization building a global climate movement through grassroots organizing and mass public actions.

Bibliography

Brandt, Allan M. "Inventing Conflicts of Interest: A
History of Tobacco Industry Tactics." *American
Journal of Public Health*, January 2012. https://www.
ncbi.nlm.nih.gov/pmc/articles/PMC3490543.

El-Hai, Jack. "In 1975, *Newsweek* Predicted a New Ice Age.
We're Still Living with the Consequences." *Longreads*,
April 2017. https://longreads.com/2017/04/13/
in-1975-newsweek-predicted-a-new-ice-age-
were-still-living-with-the-consequences.

Gatehouse, Jonathon. "The Nature of David Suzuki."
Maclean's, November 18, 2013. http://www.macleans.
ca/society/life/the-nature-of-david-suzuki.

Goldstein, Joshua S., and Steven Pinker. "Inconvenient
Truths for the Environmental Movement."
Boston Globe, November 23, 2015. https://
www.bostonglobe.com/opinion/2015/11/23/
inconvenient-truths-for-environmental-movement/
esDloe97894keW16Ywa9MP/story.html.

Gore, Al. *An Inconvenient Truth: The Planetary
Emergency of Global Warming and What We Can
Do About It*. New York: Rodale, 2006.

Government of Canada. *The Science of Climate Change*. November 23, 2015. https://www.ec.gc. ca/Publications/CDFE86EB-E309-4C4E-80EE-9D2919EEE2F9/EN---Climate-Science-Briefing---23-NOV-2015---FINAL.PDF.

Henson, Robert. *The Thinking Person's Guide to Climate Change*. Boston, MA: American Meteorological Society, 2014.

Howe, Joshua P. *Behind the Curve: Science and the Politics of Global Warming*. Seattle, WA: University of Washington Press, 2016.

Kolbert, Elizabeth. "The Catastrophist." *New Yorker*, June 29, 2009. http://www.newyorker.com/ magazine/2009/06/29/the-catastrophist.

———. *Field Notes from a Catastrophe*. New York: Bloomsbury, 2006.

Lapowsky, Issie. "Ten Years After *An Inconvenient Truth*, Al Gore May Actually Be Winning." *Wired*, May 24, 2016. https://www.wired. com/2016/05/wired-al-gore-climate-change.

McKibben, Bill, ed. *The Global Warming Reader: A Century of Writing About Climate Change*. New York: Penguin, 2012.

———. "Global Warming's Terrifying New Math: Three Simple Numbers that Add up to Global Catastrophe." *Rolling Stone*, July 19, 2012.

http://www.rollingstone.com/politics/news/global-warmings-terrifying-new-math-20120719.

Meyer, Robinson. "What's Next for the Keystone XL Pipeline?" *The Atlantic*, March 27, 2017. https://www.theatlantic.com/science/archive/2017/03/whats-next-for-the-keystone-xl-pipeline/520917.

Mooney, Chris. "Global Warming Is Now Slowing Down the Circulation of the Oceans—with Potentially Dire Consequences." *Washington Post*, March 23, 2015. https://www.washingtonpost.com/news/energy-environment/wp/2015/03/23/global-warming-is-now-slowing-down-the-circulation-of-the-oceans-with-potentially-dire-consequences/?utm_term=.34c81784d04c.

Moore, Berrien III, and Sean Crowell. "Watching the Planet Breathe." *The Conversation*, April 11, 2017. https://theconversation.com/watching-the-planet-breathe-studying-earths-carbon-cycle-from-space-72344.

Moore, David W. "Katrina Hurt Blacks and Poor Victims Most." Gallup, October 25, 2005. http://www.gallup.com/poll/19405/katrina-hurt-blacks-poor-victims-most.aspx.

Norton, Clark. "Green Giant." *Washington Post*, September 3, 1989. https://www.washingtonpost.com/archive/lifestyle/magazine/1989/09/03/green-giant/1dc78745-b567-4da6-ae97-16f9d0d0ffd1/?utm_term=.64b2a91a4df3.

Oreskes, Naomi, and Erik M. Conway. *Merchants of Doubt: How a Handful of Scientists Obscured the Truth on Issues from Tobacco Smoke to Global Warming*. New York: Bloomsbury, 2010.

Peters, E. Kirsten. *The Whole Story of Climate Change: What Science Reveals About the Nature of Endless Change*. Amherst, NY: Prometheus Books, 2012.

Roach, John. "Global Warming May Alter Atlantic Currents, Study Says." *National Geographic News*, June 27, 2005. http://news.nationalgeographic.com/news/2005/06/0627_050627_oceancurrent.html.

Shabecoff, Philip. "Global Warming Has Begun, Expert Tells Senate." *New York Times*, June 24, 1988. http://www.nytimes.com/1988/06/24/us/global-warming-has-begun-expert-tells-senate.html?pagewanted=all.

United Nations Framework Convention on Climate Change. *The Paris Agreement*. http://unfccc.int/paris_agreement/items/9485.php.

US Environmental Protection Agency. *Climate Change Indicators in the United States, 2016*. Fourth Edition. http://www.epa.gov/climate-indicators.

Weart, Spencer. *The Discovery of Global Warming: Revised and Expanded Edition*. Boston: Harvard University Press, 2008.

White, Gillian B. "A Long Road Home: The Systems in Place to Provide Aid After Natural Disasters Often Fail Those Who Need Help the Most." *The Atlantic*, August 3, 2015. https://www.theatlantic.com/business/archive/2015/08/hurricane-katrina-sandy-disaster-recovery-/400244.

Wogan, David. "Why We Know About the Greenhouse Effect." *Scientific American: Plugged In*, May 16, 2013. https://blogs.scientificamerican.com/plugged-in/why-we-know-about-the-greenhouse-gas-effect.

World Bank. "Rapid Climate-Informed Development Needed to Keep Climate Change from Pushing More Than 100 Million People into Poverty by 2030." November 8, 2015. http://www.worldbank.org/en/news/feature/2015/11/08/rapid-climate-informed-development-needed-to-keep-climate-change-from-pushing-more-than-100-million-people-into-poverty-by-2030.

Index

Page numbers in **boldface** are illustrations. Entries in **boldface** are glossary terms.

acidity, 38
aerosol, 21
Agassiz, Louis, 11, 13
algae, 35, 37, 49
allergies, 48
Antarctica, 6, 18, **33**, 35, 37
anthropogenic, 31
Arrhenius, Svante, 15
astrobiology, 95, 97

birds, 35, 39, 43, 54
Bush, George W., 85, 89

Callendar, Guy Stewart, 15–16, 69
carbon cycle, 23
carbon dioxide, 6, 13–16, 18–25, 27, 29, 31, 38, 68–69, 77, 79–80, 84–85
cardiovascular, 74
Carter, Jimmy, 22, **83**, 84
Charney, Jule, 22, 24

Charpentier, Johann von, 11, 13
China, 68–69, 84–85, 87, 89, 94
chlorofluorocarbons, 25
civil disobedience, 54, 56
Clean Air Act, 66
clean energy, 56, 77, **83**, 84, **86**, 89, 92, 94–95, 97
climate change
    causes of, 6–7, 15, 18, 23, 25, 27, 30–32, 51–53, 64–65, 68, 74, 78–80
    denial of, 5, 7, 9, 76–77, 79–80, 82, 84–85, 89, 92
    impact of, 7, 16, 22, 24, 32, 34–35, 37–39, 41, 43–44, 48–49, 58–60
    politics and, 7, 22, 25, 57–58, 62, 66, 69, 80, 82, 84–85, 87, 89–90, 92–95
    prevention of, 9, 56–58, 60, 62, 64–66, 68–69, 87, 89–90, **91**, 92–95, 97
    study of, 5–7, 9, 11, 13–16, 18–22, **19**, 24–25, 27,

30–32, **33**, 34, 47, 49, 53, 74, 78–90, 95

climate justice, 58–60

coal, 6, 15, 23, 77, 80, 82, 92, 94

consensus, 30, 72, 78–79, 89

cooling, 14, 21–22

corals, 21, 35, **36**, 37–38

dark money, 82

deforestation, 6, 31, 56, 62

demonstrations, 9, **50**, 51–54, 56–58, 64, 90, **91**, 92

drought, 16, 24, **42**, 43–44, 59

Earth Day, **50**, 51–53, 58–59, 66, 90, **91**, 92

Earth Sciences Sector (ESS), 32, 34

element, 23

Environmental Protection Agency (EPA), 34, 57, 66, 68, 84, 89

exponentially, 18

extinction, 52

ExxonMobil, **73**, 79–80, 82, 84, 92

famine, 16

First World Climate Conference, 68

fish, 11, 35, **36**, 37–39

flooding, 24, 37–39, 43, 59

fossil fuels, 6–7, 15–16, 18, 23, 27, 30, 52, 56–58, 65, 76–77, 79–80, 82, 89, 90, 92, 94

Fourier, Joseph, 14

gag order, 90

geneticist, 60

germinate, 48

glaciers, 5, 11, 13, 21, 34, 37–39, 47

Goldilocks zone, 14

Gore, Al, 53, 62, **63**, 66

greenhouse effect, 14–16, 18, 22, 25, 27, 31–32, 38, 92

Greenland, 6, 24, **28**, 37

Greenpeace, 53–54, **55**, 56

growing season, 48

Hansen, James, 25, 27, 80

Harper, Stephen, 85

ice ages, 13, 16, 21–22, 27, 39

ice sheets, 6, 20, 24, **28**, **33**, 37, **96**

illnesses, 48–49, 60

Industrial Revolution, 6, 22, 87

inoculate, 81

Intergovernmental Panel on Climate Change (IPCC), 29–32, 53, 68

Katrina, Hurricane, 59
Keeling, Charles David, 18–21, 29
Keystone XL pipeline, 56–58, 90
Kimmel, Kenneth, 82
Koch Industries, 82
krill, 35, 37
Kyoto Protocol, 68–69, 80, 84–85

Larsen C ice shelf, 37
Lennox Island, **40**, 41
lobbyist, 69, 84, 92
Lyme disease, 48–49

Mauna Loa, 18, 20
McKibben, Bill, 57
methane, 25
modeling, 22, 24–25, 27, 31, 79, 95
moraine, 11
moratorium, 90
mosquitos, 49
Muir, John, 56

NASA, 25, 34–35, 59
natural disasters, 16, 24, 37, 41, 44, 58–60
natural gas, 80, 92, 94
Natural Resources Defense Council, 58
Nelson, Gaylord, 52
Nixon, Richard, 66, 82, 84
nuclear tests, 53–54, 56

Obama, Barack, 57, 87, **88**, 89
oceans, 6, 14, 16, 18, 21–23, 27, 35, 37–39, 44, 49, 54, 56, 79
oil, 6, 23, 52, 56–57, 72, 77, 79, 90, 92

Paris Climate Agreement, 69, 87, **88**, 89–90, 92, 94–95
Peabody Energy, 80, 82
peer review, 74, 76, 78
Perraudin, Jean-Pierre, 11
pollen, 21, 48
precipitation, 43–44
Pruitt, Scott, 89

Reagan, Ronald, 84
red knots, 39, 43
Revelle, Roger, 16, **17**, 18
rhetoric, 90, 94

Roosevelt, Franklin, 71–72
Roosevelt, Theodore, 84

Sahara Desert, 31
sea levels, 24, 37–39, 41, 58
seal hunting, 54
Sierra Club, 56–57
snow, 34, 39, 43
solar activity, 27
solar energy, **83**, 84,
    86, 89, 94, 97
Suess, Hans, 18
Suzuki, David, 60, **61**, 62

teach-ins, 52–53
350.org, 57
Tillerson, Rex, 92
tobacco, 72, 74, 76, 80
toxic waste, 54, 58
Trudeau, Justin, 89–90
Trump, Donald, 57,
    69, 89–90, 92
Tyndall, John, 14–15

Union of Concerned
    Scientists, 58,
    64–65, 80, 82

vegetarianism, 64–65
Vietnam War, 52, 68, 93
volcanoes, 6, 14, 27

whaling, 54
wildfires, 48
wind energy, 77, 94, 97
World War II, 71–72

About the Author

Avery Elizabeth Hurt is the author of many books for children and young adults. When she was in high school, she won a first-place ribbon for a science fair project on dangers to the environment. Researching the project convinced her of the importance of fighting to protect our environment, and she has been doing so ever since. Though she never dreamed she would still be fighting these battles so many years later, she is very optimistic about the future of our world.